Friday Stories
Haiti 2

Henry Lea
School
Ms. Melange
Grade 6
2019

Jenny Delacruz
Illustrations by Danko Herrera

Printed in the United States of America

First Edition, 2021

ISBN: 978-1-7361533-1-4 Paperback
ISBN: 978-1-7361533-2-1 Hardcover
ISBN: 978-1-7361533-3-8 eBook

This book is dedicated to Haiti
and the language of Haitian Creole.
Your story will be remembered.

Everyone loves Fridays in Ms. Mélange's sixth-grade class because each Friday, Ms. Mélange takes her students on an exciting adventure in world history. Last week, they began exploring Haiti's history. They learned about the Haitian people's Taíno ancestry, the impact of slavery, and how Haiti gained independence while leading the world's first successful Black slave revolution. Let's join Ms. Mélange and her sixth graders as they continue exploring Haitian history. In today's class, they will discuss what happened after Haiti gained independence. Students will hear more from Jean, whose family emigrated from Haiti. Jean is very excited to share his family's perspective with his friends in Ms. Mélange's class.

Those are some good points. And unfortunately, the class system in Haiti continued after its independence. Caste or class systems are typically created to divide a group of people and maintain power. For example, before the 19th century, people in the U.S. identified as Polish, Yoruba, Irish, Igbo, Native American, and so forth. But then the main two classifications became Black and White. Since Black was associated with slavery, other groups that migrated to the U.S. did not want to be associated with blackness. Did anyone learn or read about what happened to the Dominican Republic after it declared independence?

True, Nia. Although Haiti was technically independent, it soon began to lose control with the rise of American **imperialism**. The U.S. noticed the influence of Germany and Arab countries by their migration to Haiti, and they were threatened by their increase of power and wealth.

From 1911–1915, eight Haitian presidents were assassinated. Many blamed this instability on the class divisions between the Haitian mulattoes and Arab Haitians in the south versus the Haitians in the north. From 1915 to 1934,[1] the United States used this instability to justify taking over all Haitian governmental decisions, which allowed the U.S. to rewrite the constitution of Haiti with the goal of protecting their financial investments.

What? How could the U.S. rewrite Haiti's laws if it's independent? Aren't there laws that stop countries from taking over other countries?

Actually, the United Nations, or UN, is now responsible for enforcing international laws, but the UN was not created until 1945. The new constitution, written by the United States, did not benefit the Haitian people or Haiti as a country. It created a labor force of Haitians that unfairly obligated many of them to work for American companies that did not always have Haiti's best interests in mind. Then, the U.S. established Haiti's police force to initially protect their businesses. The Haitians distrusted its establishment from the start. The U.S. took $500,000 in gold from the Haitian National Bank and transferred the money to a bank in New York for 'safekeeping.' But this move really just gave the U.S. more control over Haiti.

Well, from what my parents have told me, it got a lot worse. I heard stories about the horrors of the Reign of Terror, when Papa Doc Duvalier and then his son Baby Doc, took control of Haiti. They created a military force to terrorize everyone. People called the military enforcers the "Tonton Macoute," which means "boogie man."

My parents said that they always had to stay inside as kids because my grandparents were worried about their safety. They only traveled to the three L's: 'lakay, legliz, and lekòl,' which pretty much means your 'house, church, and school'.

As a result of the fallen economy, countless Haitians became migrant farmers in the Dominican Republic to sustain themselves and their families. But Dominicans could easily identify Haitians by their darker skin color and often treated Haitians more harshly. Unfortunately, Haitians and Dominicans continue to have these sorts of issues today.

That's **colorism**, and it's wrong! People shouldn't be judged based on their skin tones."

You're right, Isabella. It is wrong. Unfortunately, it's assumed that the lighter your skin color is, the better off you are in society. Colorism is still an issue in many nations today, including the U.S., but people are becoming more aware of it. Dark skin tones are being highlighted more in the media, and there are more discussions about accepting people regardless of the shade of their skin.

JEAN-BERTNAR
ARISTIDE

27

Then the bell rang!

As the students left the classroom, they continued their conversation about the history of Haiti wondering how the nation may or may not have changed after democracy..

300 BCE- Farming villages were established by the Ciboney and Taíno (Arawak).

1492 Christopher Columbus landed on the island and named it Little Spain, or Hispaniola.

1514 The majority of the Ciboney and Taíno population were wiped out.

1801 A former black slave, Toussaint Louverture, conquers Haiti and ends slavery.

1804 Haiti becomes the 1st Black republic in the world and Jean-Jacques Dessalines declares himself emperor.

1915 -1934 Meanwhile, the United States invaded Haiti, and Haiti gave the U.S. the power to make governmental decisions. The U.S rewrote the constitution of Haiti and maintained fiscal control until 1947.

1957-1986 Reign of Terror- Dictatorships of François "Papa Doc" Duvalier and his son Jean-Claude "Baby Doc "plundered Haiti's national treasury and terrorized the country with the Tonton Macoute, resulting in a mass migration of Haitians.

1517 The first group of enslaved Africans were brought to Hispanolia.

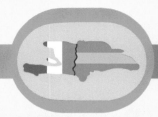

1697 Spain cedes the western part of Hispaniola to France, and this becomes Saint Domingue while the eastern part is called Santo Domingo.

1845-1947 Haiti paid France over one billion dollars in reparations.

1914-The Wilson administration sent U.S. Marines into Haiti. They removed $500,000 from the Haitian National Bank to The National City Bank of New York.

1986-Mass Uprisings ended the Duvalier Dictatorships.

1986-1990-About 8 coups took place during the rule of the Conseil National de Gouvernement (CNG), Haiti's army led government. They were known as the "New Tonton Macoute."

1990-Jean Aristide became the first democratically elected president of Haiti with the support of the UN. **31**

Reflective Questions

1. Choose a character who shares information about Haiti. What do you think about the comments they made?

2. Share what you think the children felt at the following points in the lesson:

   a. When learning about reparations

   b. When discussing bullies

   c. When learning about Papa Doc and Baby Doc

   d. When learning about Haitians who fled the country and ended up sending money back to loved ones (see pages 24-25).

3. What lessons can we learn from Haiti's history?

4. What are some creative ways you can raise awareness about Haiti's history or current events in Haiti?

Glossary

Autonomy – a self-governing state; the right of self-government.

Colorism – prejudice or discrimination, especially within a racial or ethnic group favoring people with lighter skin over those with darker skin.

Caste system – a division of society based on one an established class structure.

Disenfranchised – deprived of some right, privilege, or immunity.

Empowered – having the knowledge, confidence, means, or ability to do things or make decisions for oneself.

Gross National Income – the earnings from a nation's current production, including compensation of employees, interest, rental income, and profits of business after taxes.

Imperialism – the policy, practice, or advocacy of extending the power and dominion of a nation, especially by direct territorial acquisitions or by gaining indirect control over the political or economic life of other areas.

Inauguration – a ceremonial induction into office.

Middle Class – the social class whose members are neither very rich nor very poor. It includes professional and business people.

Reparations – monetary or other compensation payable by a country to an individual, group, or other nation for a historical wrong.

References

Abdul, Rob. *Taíno: Indigenous Caribbeans*. Black History 365, December 2, 2016. www.blackhistorymonth.org.uk/article/section/pre-colonial-history/taino-indigenous-caribbeans/. Accessed May 5, 2021.

"Autonomy." *Merriam-Webster.com Dictionary*, Merriam-Webster, www.merriam-webster.com/dictionary/autonomy. Accessed May 5, 2021.

Baptiste, N. "Terror, Repression, and Diaspora: The Baby Doc Legacy in Haiti." *The Nation*, October 23, 2014. www.thenation.com/article/archive/terror-repression-and-diaspora-baby-doc-legacy-haiti/.

Britannica. "Haiti." www.britannica.com/place/Haiti/Early-period. Accessed March 24, 2021.

"Colorism." *Merriam-Webster.com Dictionary*, Merriam-Webster, https://www.merriam-webster.com/dictionary/colorism. Accessed May 5, 2021.

"Disenfranchised." *Merriam-Webster.com Dictionary*, Merriam-Webster, https://www.merriam-webster.com/dictionary/disenfranchised. Accessed May 5, 2021.

"Empowered." *Merriam-Webster.com Dictionary*, Merriam-Webster, https://www.merriam-webster.com/dictionary/empowered. Accessed May 5, 2021.

Farmer, Paul. *Haiti after the earthquake*. Public Affairs, 2012.

Gaffield, Julia. *Haitian Connections in the Atlantic World*: Recognition after Revolution. University of North Carolina Press, 2015.

Gates, Henry Louis. *Black in Latin America: Episode 1* [DVD]. PBS, Inkwell Films/Wall to Wall Productions, 2001.

"Gross National income." *Merriam-Webster.com Dictionary*, Merriam-Webster, https://www.merriam-webster.com/dictionary/national%20income.

"Imperialism." *Merriam-Webster.com Dictionary*, Merriam-Webster, https://www.merriam-webster.com/dictionary/imperialism. Accessed May 5, 2021.

"Inauguration." *Merriam-Webster.com Dictionary*, Merriam-Webster, https://www.merriam-webster.com/dictionary/inauguration. Accessed May 5, 2021.

Kean, Katherine, Babeth, Perry Hart, and Rudi Stern. *Haiti: Killing the Dream*. Crowing Rooster Arts, 1992.

"Middle Class". *Oxford.com Dictionary*, Oxford, https://www.oxfordlearnersdictionaries.com/us/definition/english/middle-class. Accessed May 5, 2021.

Renda, Mary A. T*aking Haiti: Military Occupation & the Culture of U.S. Imperialism, 1915–1940*. University of North Carolina Press, 2004.

"Reparation." *Merriam-Webster.com Dictionary*, Merriam-Webster, https://www.merriam-webster.com/dictionary/reparation. Accessed May 5, 2021.

Shamsie, Yasmine and Andrew S. Thompson, editors. *Haiti: Hope for a Fragile State*. Wilfrid Laurier University Press, 2006.

Sidder, Aaron. "How Cholera Spread So Quickly Through Haiti." *National Geographic*, August 18, 2016. www.nationalgeographic.com/science/article/haiti-cholera-crisis-united-nations-admission. Accessed May 5, 2021.

Sperling, Dan. "In 1825, Haiti Paid France $21 Billion To Preserve Its Independence." *Forbes*, December 16, 2017. www.forbes.com/sites/realspin/2017/12/06/in-1825-haiti-gained-independence-from-france-for-21-billion-its-time-for-france-to-pay-it-back/?sh=464d5856312b. Accessed May 5, 2021.

UNESCO. "Haiti (Saint-Domingue)." http://slaveryandremembrance.org/articles/article/?id=A0111. Accessed May 5, 2021.

About the Author

Jenny Delacruz is a Haitian-American writer, a licensed counselor, and the founder of Cobbs Creek Publishing. She enjoys spending time with her husband and their two sons. Jenny was born and raised in New York where she learned the importance of diversity and that each person's story weaves back many generations.

In her counseling practice, Jenny specializes in family conflicts, trauma, grief, and parenting issues. Jenny is also a philanthropist who advocates for human rights. Her passion for teaching her children about world history and current events inspired her to pursue writing and launch her own educational children's book series. Her previous books include *Friday Stories Learning About Haiti* and *How Was Your Summer: Fostering Critical Conversations with Students*. Her most recent book, *Momma, Can I Sleep with You Tonight?* helps children cope with the impact of COVID-19 and is also available in French and Spanish.

If you want to discover more of Jenny Delacruz's work, visit her online at www.cobbscreekpublishing.com. She can also be found on Instagram and Facebook @cobbscreekpublishing.

About the Illustrator

Danko Herrera draws his inspiration from nature and landscapes. He is versatile in many drawing styles through his poetic and detailed use of colors and lines.

He has worked for various environmental, educational, commercial organizations, and businesses as an illustrator, and his art has also appeared in murals, bestselling books, and art festivals around the world in countries like Denmark, Argentina, the United States, and Mexico.

Visit his website at danko.mx, and follow him on Instagram @danko.mx.

CPSIA information can be obtained
at www.ICGtesting.com
Printed in the USA
BVHW091554141221
624017BV00007B/537